SERMON
ON THE MOUNT

JEN WILKIN

LifeWay Press®
Nashville, Tennessee

Published by LifeWay Press ® • © 2014 Jen Wilkin

Reprinted September 2018

ISBN: 978-1-4300-3228-1

Item: 005644876

Dewey Decimal Classification: 226.9

Subject Headings: SERMON ON THE MOUNT \ KINGDOM OF GOD \ SPIRITUAL LIFE

Scripture quotations are from The Holy Bible, English Standard Version® (ESV®), copyright © 2001 by Crossway, a publishing ministry of Good News Publishers. Used by permission. All rights reserved.

Scripture taken from the Holy Bible, NEW INTERNATIONAL VERSION®. Copyright © 1973, 1978, 1984 by Biblica, Inc. All rights reserved worldwide. Used by permission.

To order additional copies of this resource, order online at *www.lifeway.com*; write LifeWay Small Groups: One LifeWay Plaza, Nashville, TN 37234-0152; fax order to 615.251.5933; or call toll-free 1.800.458.2772.

Printed in the United States of America

Adult Ministry Publishing
LifeWay Church Resources
One LifeWay Plaza
Nashville, TN 37234-0152

PRODUCTION TEAM

WRITER:
JEN WILKIN

EDITORIAL PROJECT LEADER:
BRIAN DANIEL

CONTENT EDITOR:
GENA ROGERS

PRODUCTION EDITOR:
MEGAN HAMBY

VIDEO PRODUCERS & DIRECTORS:
TIM COX
HAL SANDIFER

VIDEO ASSISTANT PRODUCER:
LISA TURNER

VIDEO EDITOR:
TIM COX

ART DIRECTOR:
JON RODDA

DIRECTOR, ADULT MINISTRY:
FAITH WHATLEY

DIRECTOR, ADULT MINISTRY PUBLISHING:
PHILIP NATION

CONTENTS

ABOUT THE GOSPEL COALITION

The Gospel Coalition is a fellowship of evangelical churches deeply committed to renewing our faith in the gospel of Christ and to reforming our ministry practices to conform fully to the Scriptures. We have become deeply concerned about some movements within traditional evangelicalism that seem to be diminishing the church's life and leading us away from our historic beliefs and practices. On the one hand, we are troubled by the idolatry of personal consumerism and the politicization of faith; on the other hand, we are distressed by the unchallenged acceptance of theological and moral relativism. These movements have led to the easy abandonment of both biblical truth and the transformed living mandated by our historic faith. We not only hear of these influences, we see their effects. We have committed ourselves to invigorating churches with new hope and compelling joy based on the promises received by grace alone through faith alone in Christ alone.

We believe that in many evangelical churches a deep and broad consensus exists regarding the truths of the gospel. Yet we often see the celebration of our union with Christ replaced by the age-old attractions of power and affluence, or by monastic retreats into ritual, liturgy, and sacrament. What replaces the gospel will never promote a mission-hearted faith anchored in enduring truth working itself out in unashamed discipleship eager to stand the tests of kingdom-calling and sacrifice. We desire to advance along the King's highway, always aiming to provide gospel advocacy, encouragement, and education so that current- and next-generation church leaders are better equipped to fuel their ministries with principles and practices that glorify the Savior and do good to those for whom He shed His life's blood.

We want to generate a unified effort among all peoples—an effort that is zealous to honor Christ and multiply His disciples, joining in a true coalition for Jesus. Such a biblically grounded and united mission is the only enduring future for the church. This reality compels us to stand with others who are stirred by the conviction that the mercy of God in Jesus Christ is our only hope of eternal salvation. We desire to champion this gospel with clarity, compassion, courage, and joy—gladly linking hearts with fellow believers across denominational, ethnic, and class lines.

Our desire is to serve the church we love by inviting all of our brothers and sisters to join us in an effort to renew the contemporary church in the ancient gospel of Christ so we truly speak and live for Him in a way that clearly communicates to our age. As pastors, we intend to do this in our churches through the ordinary means of His grace: prayer, ministry of the Word, baptism and the Lord's

Supper, and the fellowship of the saints. We yearn to work with all who seek the lordship of Christ over the whole of life with unabashed hope in the power of the Holy Spirit to transform individuals, communities, and cultures.

In its Women's Initiatives, The Gospel Coalition aims for gospel renewal specifically among and through the women of the church. We desire to support the growth of women in faithfully studying and sharing the Scriptures; in actively loving and serving the church; and in spreading the gospel of Jesus Christ in all their callings. Women benefit from and contribute to The Gospel Coalition's resources in many ways—on the website, in conference settings, and in various publishing projects. We pray that, through the Women's Initiatives, Jesus will be glorified and the church will be strengthened.

FOREWORD

HOW SHOULD WE APPROACH GOD'S WORD?

OUR PURPOSE

The Bible study you are about to begin may be different from studies you have done in the past. It will not cover a specific topic from many angles. It will not have poetry or stories that leave you laughing, crying, or inspired. It will not focus on answering the question, "What does the Bible say about me?" It will not aid you in self-discovery, at least not as its primary intent.

What it will do is teach you an important passage of the Bible in a way that will stay with you for years to come. It will challenge you to move beyond loving God with just your heart to loving Him with your mind. It will focus on answering the question, "What does the Bible say about God?" It will aid you in the worthy task of God-discovery.

You see, the Bible isn't a book about self-discovery; it's a book about God-discovery. The Bible is God's declared intent to make Himself known to us. In learning about the character of God in Scripture we will experience self-discovery, but it must not be the focus of our study. The focus must be God Himself.

This focus changes the way we study. We look first for what a passage can teach us about the character of God, allowing self-discovery to be the by-product of God-discovery. This is a much better approach because there can be no true knowledge of self apart from knowledge of God. So when I read the account of Jonah, I see first that God is just and faithful to His Word; He is faithful to proclaim His message to Nineveh no matter what. I see second that I, by contrast (and much like Jonah), am unjust to my fellow man and unfaithful to God's Word. Thus knowledge of God leads to true knowledge of self, which leads to repentance and transformation. This is what Paul meant when he wrote that we are transformed by the renewing of our minds (see Rom. 12:2).

Women are good at loving God with their hearts. We are good at engaging our emotions in our pursuit of God. But the God who commands us to love with the totality of our heart, soul, and strength also commands us to love Him with all of our minds. God only commands what He also enables His children to do. Therefore, it must be possible for us to love Him well with our minds, or He would not command it. I know you will bring your emotions to your study of God's Word, and that is good and right. But it's your mind I want to engage. God intends for you to be a good student, renewing your mind and thus transforming your heart.

OUR PROCESS

Being a good student entails following good study habits. When we sit down to read, most of us like to read through a particular passage and then find a way to apply it to our everyday lives. We may read through an entire book of the Bible over a period of time, or we may jump around from place to place. I want to suggest a different approach, one that may not always yield immediate application, comfort, or peace, but one that builds over time a cumulative understanding of the message of Scripture.

Imagine receiving a letter in the mail. The envelope is hand-written, but you don't glance at the return address. Instead you tear open the envelope, flip to the second page, read two paragraphs near the bottom, and set the letter aside. Knowing someone took the time to send it to you, you spend a few minutes trying to figure out how to respond to what the section you just read had to say. What are the odds you will be successful?

No one would read a letter this way. But this is precisely the way many of us read our Bibles. We skip past reading the "envelope"—Who wrote this? To whom is it written? When was it written? Where was it written?—and try to determine the purpose of its contents from a portion of the whole. What if we took time to read the envelope? What if, after determining the context for its writing, we started at the beginning and read to the end? Wouldn't that make infinitely more sense?

In our study we will take this approach with Scripture. We will begin by placing our text in its historical and cultural context. We will "read the envelope." Then we will read through the entire text multiple times, so we can better determine what it wants to say to us. We will read repetitively so we might move through three critical stages of understanding: comprehension, interpretation, and application.

Stage 1: Comprehension

Remember the reading comprehension section on the SAT? Remember those long reading passages followed by questions to test your knowledge of what you had just read? The objective was to force you to read for detail. We're going to apply the same method to our study of God's Word. When we read for comprehension we ask ourselves, "What does it say?" This is hard work. A person who comprehends the account of the six days of creation can tell you specifically what happened on each day. This is the first step toward being able to interpret and apply the story of creation to our lives.

Stage 2: Interpretation

Comprehension asks, "What does it say?" Interpretation asks, "What does it mean?" Once we have read a passage enough times to know what it says, we are ready to look into its meaning. A person who interprets the creation story can tell you why God created the world in a particular order or way. They are able to infer things from the text beyond what it says.

Stage 3: Application

After doing the work to understand what the text says and what the text means, we are finally ready to ask, "How should it change me?" Here is where we draw on our God-centered perspective to ask three supporting questions:

- What does this passage teach me about God?
- How does this aspect of God's character change my view of self?
- What should I do in response?

A person who applies the creation story can tell us that because God creates in an orderly fashion, we too should live well-ordered lives. Knowledge of God gleaned through comprehension of the text and interpretation of its meaning can now be applied to our lives in a way that challenges us to be different.

SOME GUIDELINES

It's vital to the learning process that you allow yourself to move through the three stages of understanding on your own, without the aid of commentaries or study notes. The first several times you read a passage you will probably be confused. This is actually a good thing. Allow yourself to feel lost, to dwell in the "I don't know." It will make the moment of discovery stick.

Nobody likes to feel lost or confused, but it's an important step in the acquisition and retention of understanding. Because of this, I have a few guidelines to lay out for you as you go through this study:

I. Avoid all commentaries until comprehension and interpretation have been earnestly attempted on your own. In other words, wait to read commentaries until after you have done the homework, attended small-group time, and watched the video teaching. And then, consult commentaries you can trust. Visit *www.mystudybible.com* for suggestions.

II. For the purposes of this study, get a Bible without study notes. Come on, it's just too easy to look at them. You know I'm right.

III. Though commentaries are off-limits, here are some tools you should use:

- *Cross-references*. These are the Scripture references in the margin or at the bottom of the page in your Bible. They point you to other passages that deal with the same topic or theme.
- *An English dictionary* to look up unfamiliar words.
- *Other translations of the Bible*. We will use the English Standard Version (ESV) as a starting point, and the New International Version (NIV) as our secondary translation. You can easily consult other versions online. Reading a passage in more than one translation can expand your understanding of its meaning. **Note:** A paraphrase, such as The Message, can be useful but should be regarded as a commentary rather than a translation. Paraphrases are best consulted after careful study of an actual translation.
- *A printed copy of the text*, double-spaced, so you can mark repeated words, phrases, or ideas. The entire text for this study is provided in the appendix of your workbook in the ESV translation.

STORING UP TREASURE

Approaching God's Word with a God-centered perspective, with context, and with care takes effort and commitment. It's study for the long-term. Some days your study may not move you emotionally or speak to an immediate need. You may not be able to apply a passage at all. But what if 10 years from now, in a dark night of the soul, that passage suddenly opens up to you because of the work you have done today? Wouldn't your long-term investment be worth it?

In Matthew 13, we see Jesus teach in parables. He tells seven deceptively simple stories that leave His disciples struggling for understanding— dwelling in the "I don't know," if you will. After the last parable He turns to them and asks, "Have you understood all these things?" Despite their apparent confusion, they answer out of their earnest desire with "Yes." Jesus told them that their newfound understanding makes them "like the owner of a house who brings out of his store-room new treasures as well as old" (Matt. 13:52, NIV).

A storeroom is a place for keeping valuables over a long period of time for use when needed. Faithful study of God's Word is a means for filling our spiritual storerooms with truth, so that in our hour of need we can bring forth both the old and the new as a source of rich provision. I pray that this study would be for you a source of much treasure, and that you would labor well to obtain it.

Grace and peace,

Jen Wilkin

HOW TO USE THIS STUDY

This workbook is designed to be used in a specific way. The homework will start you down the process of comprehension, interpretation, and application. However, it was designed to dovetail with small-group discussion time and the video teaching. You can use the workbook by itself, but you are likely to find yourself with some unresolved questions. The video teaching is intended to resolve most, if not all, of your unanswered questions from the homework and discussion time. With this in mind, consider using the materials as follows:

- If you are going through the study on your own, first work through the homework and then watch the corresponding teaching video for that week. See *lifeway.com/sermononthemount*.
- If you are going through the study in a group, first do your homework, then discuss the questions your group decides to cover, and then watch the video teaching.

Note: For week 1 there is no homework. The study begins with a video introduction. You will find a viewer guide on pages 12-13 that you can use as you watch the introductory message.

A MESSAGE FOR GROUP LEADERS ═══

At the end of each week's personal study you will find discussion questions to help you facilitate your small-group time. Each begins with an introductory question to help group members get to know one another and feel comfortable contributing their voices to the discussion. These questions may prove to be most helpful during the early weeks of the study, but as the group grows more familiar with one another, you may decide to skip the introductory question to allow more time to discuss the questions covering the lesson.

Following the introductory question you will find four questions to help group members compare what they have learned from their personal study on days 2 through 5. These questions are either pulled directly from the personal study or they summarize a concept or theme that the personal study covered. Each two-part question covers content from a particular day of the personal study, first asking group members to reflect, and then asking them to apply. The reflection questions typically ask group members to report a finding or flesh out an interpretation. The application questions challenge them to move beyond intellectual understanding to identify ways to live differently in light of what they have learned.

As a small-group leader, you will want to review these questions before you meet with your group, thinking through your own answers, marking where the questions occur in the personal study, and noting if there are any additional questions you might want to reference to help the flow of the discussion. These questions are suggestions only, intended to help you cover as much ground as you can in your discussion time. They should not be seen as requirements or limitations, but as guidelines to help you prepare your group for the video teaching time by allowing them to process collectively what they have learned during their personal study.

As a facilitator of discussion rather than a teacher, you are allowed and encouraged to be a co-learner with your group members. This means you may not always feel confident of your answer to a given question, and that is perfectly OK. Because we are studying for the long-term, we are allowed to leave some questions partially answered or unresolved, trusting for clarity at a later time. In most cases, the video teaching time should address any lingering questions that are not resolved in the personal study or the small-group discussion.

THE KINGDOM OF
HEAVEN

MATTHEW 5:1-2

¹ Seeing the crowds, he went up on the mountain,
and when he sat down, his disciples came to him.
² And he opened his mouth and taught them, saying: …

MATTHEW 5:1-2

Why are there _____?

Who is Jesus' _____ for the Sermon on the Mount?

Primary: _____

Secondary: _____

Why does Jesus _____?

      Psalm 80:1-2   Throne

      Psalm 99:1   Throne

      Hebrews 1:3   Right hand of Majesty

Why is Jesus _____?

      Matthew 17:1-13   Transfiguration

      Matthew 24   Olivet Discourse

      Matthew 28:16-20   The Great Commission

      Exodus 19–20   God speaks on Mount Sinai

WHO

IS BLESSED?

Each week you will start your homework by reading through the entire Sermon on the Mount from start to finish. Then you'll focus in on a particular passage to discover its message and how it fits into the greater context of the sermon as a whole. By the time you complete this study, you will have read the Sermon on the Mount at least nine times. As it grows more familiar to you, watch for how your understanding deepens and expands. Your first task each week will be to note how this process is taking place. To help you read for detail, you'll be asked to mark certain words or phrases in the copy of Matthew 5–7 printed in the back of this book. Keep a set of colored pencils or markers handy as you read.

This week we'll focus our study efforts on dissecting the eight short statements that form the opening to Jesus' longest recorded message—statements commonly known as the Beatitudes. You may be familiar with some or all of them. We'll strive to look at them with fresh eyes, asking ourselves why, of all the ways Jesus could have begun His inaugural address to His disciples, He begins with a list of "blesseds."

DAY 1

Read Matthew 5:1–7:29 on pages 138-144.

As you read, circle each occurrence of the word "righteousness" with a blue pencil or marker. We will be considering its meaning and use on Day 3.

1. Which section of the sermon seems unclear to you?

    _____

    _____

    _____

2. Which section seems most straightforward?

    _____

    _____

    _____

3. Look up the word *beatitude* in the dictionary. Write the definition below:

    _____

    _____

    _____

4. Why do you think Jesus chooses to begin the Sermon on the Mount with a list of "blesseds"?

    _____

    _____

DAY 2

> [3] *Blessed are the poor in spirit, for theirs is the*
> *kingdom of heaven.*
> [4] *Blessed are those who mourn, for they*
> *shall be comforted.*
>
> **MATTHEW 5:3-4**

1. Look up the following passages and note what each teaches us about being poor:

   Psalm 40:16-17: _____

   Psalm 69:32-33: _____

   Psalm 72:12-14: _____

   Isaiah 66:2 (*humble* is translated "poor" in the KJV): _____

   What kind of poverty is addressed in these verses? _____

2. Webster's Dictionary defines *poverty* as "the state of one with insufficient resources."[1] Based on this definition, what does it mean to be "poor in spirit"?

3. What does Jesus say belongs to those who are poor in spirit?

In our video introduction in Week 1, we defined the *kingdom of heaven* as "the kingdom of grace here, and the kingdom of glory hereafter." It's the reign of God established at Christ's first coming and consummated (completed) at His second coming. It's the rule of God particularly over believers.

4. Why do you think Jesus says that the kingdom of heaven belongs to the "poor in spirit"?

5. Now look at the second Beatitude in Matthew 5:4. People can mourn for many reasons. What are some things that cause us to mourn?

6. Compare Joel 2:12-13 and James 4:7-10. What do we learn about the role of mourning in these passages?

7. In light of these passages and in light of the first Beatitude, what kind of mourning do you think Jesus is referring to when He says, "Blessed are those who mourn"?

_____

_____

8. How has recognizing your lack of spiritual resources been a blessing to you? What role has godly grief played in your repentance?

_____

_____

9. Give an example of a time each of these two blessings has operated in your life.

_____

_____

10. Rewrite (paraphrase) the first and second Beatitudes in your own words, getting as close to their intended meaning as you can.

_____

_____

DAY 3

> [5] *Blessed are the meek, for they shall inherit the earth.*
>
> [6] *Blessed are those who hunger and thirst for righteousness, for they shall be satisfied.*
>
> **MATTHEW 5:5-6**

Webster's Dictionary defines *meek* as "enduring injury with patience and without resentment."[2] A meek person is someone who is not occupied with self at all, someone who does not insist on a set of rights.

1. Read Isaiah 53. Based on this prophetic passage and on Webster's definition of the word *meek*, how did Christ perfectly demonstrate meekness?

2. How would having a true estimate of ourselves in relation to God help us be meek?

3. What would the world say is a synonym for *meek*?

   lowly,

4. How does the third Beatitude contrast with the world's opinion of who will inherit the earth?

_____

5. In what sense do you think the meek will inherit the earth?

_____

_____

6. If a meek person is someone who does not insist on a set of rights, how meek are you? What rights do you feel entitled to or take for granted in your home, church, workplace, or community?

_____

_____

7. How can a sense of entitlement stifle your relationship with God or skew your perception of God?

_____

_____

8. Now look at the fourth Beatitude in Matthew 5:6. On Day 1 you circled the word _righteousness_ with a blue pencil or marker. How many times does it occur in the sermon?   5

9. Look up the word *righteousness* in the dictionary. Write the definition below.

_____

_____

10. Look up the following passages and answer the questions for each.

John 4:7-10:
Who is speaking? _____

What is offered? _____

What need is satisfied? _____

John 6:35:
Who is speaking? _____

What is offered? _____

What need is satisfied? _____

11. Read 1 Corinthians 1:26-31. According to verse 30, who is our righteousness?

_____

12. We hunger and thirst after many things besides righteousness. What are you hungering and thirsting for right now that cannot satisfy? List your thoughts below.

_____

_____

13. In what ways are these things poor substitutes for Christ?

_____

_____

14. Rewrite (paraphrase) the third and fourth Beatitudes in your own words, getting as close to their intended meaning as you can.

_____

_____

DAY 4

> *7 Blessed are the merciful, for they shall receive mercy.*
>
> *8 Blessed are the pure in heart, for they shall see God.*
>
> **MATTHEW 5:7-8**

1. How would you define *mercy*? How does justice relate to mercy? Use a dictionary or thesaurus to help with your answer.

_____

_____

_____

2. Read Matthew 7:1-2. What concept is presented in this later passage of the Sermon on the Mount that is also presented in the fifth Beatitude?

_____

_____

3. Why do you think how we treat others will affect how God treats us?

4. To whom do you have difficulty showing mercy? How could you adjust your perspective so that showing mercy to that person becomes easier?

5. Now look at the sixth Beatitude, Matthew 5:8. Think about what Jesus means by "pure in heart." How would you respond to someone who defined "pure in heart" as sinless? Look up 1 John 1:8 to help with your answer.

6. If being pure in heart is not being perfect or free from sin, what is it?

7. Why do you think the pure in heart will "see God"?

8. Read Isaiah 6:1-8. Was Isaiah "pure in heart"? Why or why not?

9. In what specific areas of your life do you battle impurity of heart?

_____

10. How do these areas of sin cloud your ability to "see God"?

_____

_____

11. Rewrite (paraphrase) the fifth and sixth Beatitudes in your own words, getting as close to their intended meaning as you can.

_____

_____

DAY 5

> [9] Blessed are the peacemakers, for they shall be called sons of God.
> [10] Blessed are those who are persecuted for righteousness' sake, for theirs is the kingdom of heaven.
>
> **MATTHEW 5:9-10**

1. Look up the word *peacemaker* in a dictionary and write the definition below. Note any synonyms you think would fit with the way Jesus uses the word "peacemaker" in the seventh Beatitude.

_____

_____

2. Read Isaiah 9:6. Which of the titles given for Jesus relates to the seventh Beatitude?

_____

_____

3. Read Galatians 4:4-7. Based on these verses and your answer to the previous question, why do you think the peacemakers will be called the "sons of God"?

_____

_____

4. What are practical ways to be a practicing peacemaker? Think of specific ways we can use our speech and actions to be peacemakers, and note them below.

In our home: _____

In our church: _____

In our community/workplace: _____

In our country: _____

5. What is the contrast between the seventh and eighth Beatitudes? In other words, why would a peacemaker ever be the object of persecution?

_____

_____

6. For what reason does the eighth Beatitude say persecution will occur?

"for _____   _____"

7. Look back at Day 3, question 11. Who did we learn is our righteousness
    (see 1 Cor. 1:30)?

    How does Matthew 5:11 confirm this connection?

8. Have you ever been persecuted "for righteousness' sake"? Think about how the
    experience changed you. Did you feel "blessed"? Share your thoughts below.

9. Rewrite (paraphrase) the seventh and eighth Beatitudes in your own words,
    getting as close to their intended meaning as you can.

WRAP-UP

What impacted you most in this week's passage from the Sermon on the Mount?
How has Jesus challenged your concept of what it means to be "blessed"?

1. *Merriam Webster's Collegiate Dictionary*, 11th ed., s.v. "poverty."
2. *Merriam Webster's Collegiate Dictionary*, 11th ed., s.v. "meek."

GROUP DISCUSSION

INTRODUCTORY QUESTION: Describe your most memorable encounter with someone who is famous and/or wealthy. How did you respond and why?

1. **REFLECT:** Based on your Day 2 study this week, why should we desire to be poor in spirit and mourn?

   APPLY: [Day 2, questions 8-9] How has recognizing your lack of spiritual resources been a blessing to you? What role has godly grief played in your repentance? Give an example of a time each of these two blessings has operated in your life.

2. **REFLECT:** [Day 3, question 1] Based on Isaiah 53, how did Christ perfectly demonstrate meekness?

   APPLY: [Day 3, questions 6-7] If a meek person is someone who does not insist on a set of rights, how meek are you? What rights do you feel entitled to or take for granted in your home, church, workplace, or community? How can a sense of entitlement stifle your relationship with God or skew your perception of God?

3. **REFLECT:** On Day 4 we learned about being merciful and pure in heart. How are these two blessed qualities related to each other? Can we be one without being the other?

   APPLY: [Day 4, question 4] To whom do you have difficulty showing mercy? How could you adjust your perspective so that showing mercy to that person becomes easier?

4. **REFLECT:** What is a peacemaker? How was Jesus a peacemaker?

   APPLY: [Day 5, question 4] What are practical ways to be a practicing peacemaker in your home, church, community/workplace, country?

WRAP-UP: What impacted you most in this week's passage from the Sermon on the Mount? How has Jesus challenged your concept of what it means to be "blessed"?

Last week we learned whom Jesus considered blessed. We listened as He turned His disciples' expectations for what it meant to be a citizen of the kingdom of heaven upside down—rather than kings and conquerors, citizens of the kingdom should expect to be aliens and strangers. Rather than pursue a political agenda, citizens should expect to pursue a spiritual one. Rather than a kingdom established through the conquest of its rulers, citizens should expect a kingdom established through the character of its servants.

In eight simple statements, Jesus explained to His listeners where this character takes root and how it bears fruit. Character, He said, takes root in spiritual poverty, grief, submission, and famine (see Matt. 5:3-6). Character, He said, bears the fruit of compassion, purification, reconciliation, and identification (see Matt. 5:7-10). When we answer the call to discipleship, we enter into a kingdom that turns human expectations of blessedness upside down.

Having illuminated the character of the citizens of the kingdom of heaven, Jesus will now move on to examine their influence on the world around them. He does so with two simple illustrations drawn from everyday life: salt and light. And He issues a call to righteousness that will boggle the minds of those gathered to hear Him teach.

DAY 1

Read Matthew 5:1–7:29 on pages 138-144.

Circle each occurrence of the phrase "kingdom of heaven" with a red pencil or marker.

1. How many times does this phrase occur? _____

2. Has your understanding of a difficult passage improved with repeated reading this week? In what ways?

    _____

    _____

    Has a straightforward passage taken on deeper meaning for you with repeated reading this week? In what ways?

    _____

    _____

3. In Matthew 5:1-11, what is Jesus' main point? Summarize this section in a phrase or sentence.

    _____

4. In Matthew 5:13-16, what is Jesus' main point? Summarize this section in a phrase or sentence.

    _____

5. In Matthew 5:17-19, what is Jesus' main point? Summarize this section in a phrase or sentence.

    _____

DAY 2

You are the salt of the earth, but if salt has lost its taste, how shall its saltiness be restored? It is no longer good for anything except to be thrown out and trampled under people's feet.

MATTHEW 5:13

Before refrigeration, salt was used as a preservative to keep meat from rotting. In the following passages, salt is mentioned for a specific reason. Read each passage and note what you learn about salt.

Read Genesis 19:1-26.

1. What role does salt play in this passage?

   punishment

2. Why do you think Lot's wife was turned into a pillar of salt (v. 26)?

3. Why do you think salt is specifically mentioned, rather than some other substance?

   punishment

Read Leviticus 2:11-13.

4. What role does salt play in this passage?

5. Why do you think salt is specifically mentioned, rather than some other substance?

_____

_____

Compare Numbers 18:19 and 2 Chronicles 13:5.

6. What common "salty" phrase do they share?

_____

7. Why do you think God would combine the ideas of covenant and salt?

_____

_____

8. What does Jesus mean when He refers to His disciples as the "salt of the earth"?

salt prevents nothing of the world

9. What are some specific ways believers can be "salt" in this world?

_____

_____

10. What relationship in your life needs salt?

_____

_____

DAY 3

> [14] *You are the light of the world. A city set on a hill cannot be hidden.* [15] *Nor do people light a lamp and put it under a basket, but on a stand, and it gives light to all in the house.* [16] *In the same way, let your light shine before others, so that they may see your good works and give glory to your Father who is in heaven.*
>
> **MATTHEW 5:14-16**

1. What are some of the functions of light in the natural world?

   _____

   _____

2. How does the analogy of "light" illustrate the role of Jesus' disciples in the world?

   _____

   _____

3. When our light shines before men, what is it that will be noticeable about us? (Check one.)

   ☐ Our prosperous lifestyle

   ☐ The words we speak

   ☐ The good we do

   Why do you think this is so?

   _____

   _____

4. Read 1 John 1:5-7; 2:7-11. Record each phrase containing "darkness" or "light" under the appropriate heading on the chart below:

DARKNESS	LIGHT

5. In what sense is the church a light to the world?

_____

_____

6. How does the church's role as light *differ* from its role as salt?

_____

_____

7. How does the church's role as light *complement* its role as salt?

_____

_____

8. According to Matthew 5:16, how will those around us respond as we shine forth the light of truth?

_____

_____

9. Is there a specific situation in which God is calling you to be the light of truth? What holds you back from fulfilling your role as the light of the world?

_____

_____

10. Restate the following in your own words:

"You are the salt of the earth."

_____

_____

"You are the light of the world."

_____

_____

DAY 4

> [17] *Do not think that I have come to abolish the Law or the Prophets; I have not come to abolish them but to fulfill them.* [18] *For truly, I say to you, until heaven and earth pass away, not an iota, not a dot, will pass from the Law until all is accomplished.*

MATTHEW 5:17-18

1. In Matthew 5:17, Jesus addresses the silent conclusion of His disciples, based on what He told them in Matthew 5:1-16. In other words, verses 1-16 would lead the disciples to think, *Jesus means to do away with the Law and the Prophets!* Why would the disciples come to this conclusion?

2. How do Jesus' comments in Matthew 5:17-20 set up His listeners for what will follow in Matthew 5:21–6:18?

3. What was the role of a prophet in the Old Testament? (Look up the term *prophet* in a dictionary if you need a little help.) Check one answer below:

   ☐ to offer the sacrifices in the temple

   ☐ to give his interpretation of the will of God

   ☐ to serve as a mouthpiece for the words of God

4. What do you think Jesus means when He speaks of "the Law and the Prophets"? What is He referring to?

_____

_____

5. Scripture teaches that the Law is given for a threefold purpose: to reveal sin, to establish decency in society, and to provide a rule of life. Match the following verses with the use of the Law they demonstrate.

Exodus 20:12-17   The Law reveals sin.

Romans 13:8-10   The Law provides a rule of life.

Romans 3:19-20   The Law establishes decency in society.

6. Webster defines *fulfill* as "to make full: to measure up to; to satisfy."[1] In what way(s) do you think Christ fulfills each of these three aspects of the Law? Read John 8:1-11 and note below how Jesus fulfills each aspect of the law in the story related there.

THE LAW	CHRIST FULFILLS THE LAW
Reveals sin	
Establishes decency in society	
Provides a rule of life	

The Law given in Scripture can be broken into two categories: *moral law*, like the Ten Commandments, and *ceremonial law*, like the regulations found in the Book of Leviticus.

Old Testament ceremonial law was given as part of the Mosaic covenant at Mount Sinai. It served two basic purposes. First, it dictated the rules and regulations for ritual cleanliness that allowed a person to commune with a holy God. Second, it dictated regulations regarding everyday life—food, work on the Sabbath, whom one could marry—which served to distinguish the Jews from their Gentile neighbors as the chosen people of God. The Pharisees were experts in observing outwardly both the ceremonial and the moral law.

7. Read Acts 10:9-16; 11:1-18. What do Peter and the other apostles conclude from Peter's vision?

_____

_____

8. Read Mark 7:14-16. How do Jesus' words shed further light on the issue of clean and unclean things?

_____

_____

9. If "not the smallest letter, not the least stroke of a pen, will by any means disappear from the Law until everything is accomplished" (Matt 5:18, NIV), why do we no longer observe ceremonial law? Why do we no longer sacrifice animals, cleanse ourselves before worshiping, or avoid certain foods?

_____

_____

DAY 5

¹⁹ Therefore whoever relaxes one of the least of these commandments and teaches others to do the same will be called least in the kingdom of heaven, but whoever does them and teaches them will be called great in the kingdom of heaven. ²⁰ For I tell you, unless your righteousness exceeds that of the scribes and Pharisees, you will never enter the kingdom of heaven.

MATTHEW 5:19-20

1. How are we guilty of relaxing the commands of God? Give a general statement of how we do this, followed by a specific example.

2. Why do you think Jesus says those who relax God's commands and teach others to do the same will be called least in the kingdom of heaven?

3. In Matthew 5:19, Jesus states, "whoever *practices* and *teaches* these commands will be called great in the kingdom of heaven" (NIV, emphasis mine). What is the implied relationship between practicing and teaching the commands of God?

4. Who were the scribes and the Pharisees? Look up each term in the dictionary and write a definition for each that fits the historical context of this passage.

Scribe (compare the NIV to help with your definition): ⎽⎽⎽⎽⎽⎽⎽⎽⎽⎽⎽⎽

⎽⎽

Pharisee: ⎽⎽

⎽⎽

Based on your definitions, do you think the scribes and Pharisees were highly regarded or lowly regarded within society?

⎽⎽

5. In week 2, we defined *righteousness* as utter purity of character. What sort of righteousness did the scribes and Pharisees possess? Read Matthew 23:1-7 to check your answer.

⎽⎽

⎽⎽

In light of your answer above, what sort of righteousness could ever exceed that of the Pharisees?

⎽⎽

⎽⎽

6. Is there someone in your life to whom you are called to teach the commands of God? How can your actions better align with the commands you are teaching?

_____

_____

Pray and ask God to help you teach only that which you practice and practice only that which you teach.

WRAP-UP

What impacted you most in this week's passage from the Sermon on the Mount? What are the words of Jesus asking of you personally?

_____

_____

1. *Merriam Webster's Collegiate Dictionary*, 11th ed. s.v. "fulfill."

GROUP DISCUSSION

INTRODUCTORY QUESTION: Describe your biggest cooking catastrophe.

1. **REFLECT:** In the introduction to the Day 2 homework, you read that salt was primarily used as a preservative before refrigeration. Look back over the questions from Day 2. What do you think salt symbolizes in these passages?

   APPLY: [Day 2, questions 9-10] What are some specific ways believers can be "salt" in this world? What relationship in your life needs salt?

2. **REFLECT:** [Day 3, questions 1-2] What are some of the functions of light in the natural world? How does the analogy of "light" illustrate the role of Jesus' disciples in the world?

   APPLY: [Day 3, question 9] Is there a specific situation in which God is calling you to be the light of truth? What holds you back from fulfilling your role as the light of the world?

3. **REFLECT:** [Day 4, question 1] In Matthew 5:17, Jesus addresses the silent conclusion of His disciples, based on what He told them in verses 1-16. In other words, Matthew 5:1-16 would lead the disciples to think, *Jesus means to do away with the Law and the Prophets!* Why would the disciples come this conclusion?

   APPLY: Give some examples of how the Old Testament Law provides "rules of life." Are these laws still necessary? Why or why not?

4. **REFLECT:** [Day 5, question 5] What sort of righteousness could ever exceed that of the Pharisees?

   APPLY: [Day 5, question 1] How are we guilty of relaxing the commands of God? Give a general statement of how we do this, followed by a specific example.

WRAP-UP: What impacted you most in this week's passage from the Sermon on the Mount? What are the words of Jesus asking of you personally?

VIDEO

Watch the teaching video for Week 3. Use the space below to take notes.

NOTES

Matthew 5:14-16·17/5:19 5:20
  In Jesus Day Salt was
  1. valuable.
  2 Practical.
  3 useful.
Lots Wife - A love for sin. Salt cures
  Salt makes you thirsty
  Light reveals what is hidden in darkness
  Light causes things to grow
  Light shows true colors.
  Right motives + right actions

After the video concludes, close your study in prayer. Praise God for sending Christ to fulfill all righteousness on our behalf. Ask Him to show you where you have trusted in your own righteousness. Ask Him for the courage to be salt and light in your key relationships. Thank God that through the finished work of Christ, we have been given a righteousness that renders us fit for heaven.

YOU HAVE HEARD THAT

IT WAS SAID

PART 1

Last week we learned that those who follow Christ are people of influence. As spiritual salt, we prevent moral decay. And as spiritual light, we promote the growth of righteousness. We learned that Jesus did not come to do away with the Law, but to fulfill it through a deeper obedience. And we marveled with Jesus' original hearers that God required a greater righteousness than that demonstrated by the most religious people we know.

This week we will discover what Jesus means by a "righteousness [that] exceeds that of the scribes and Pharisees" (Matt. 5:20). Jesus will turn our attention to the Law itself, exploring the distance between the hypocrisy of those whose outward obedience to the law of God conceals a heart that is far from the God of the Law. If you have ever "graded yourself" on how well you follow the Ten Commandments, you may have found some comfort in at least not having broken two of them: the commands to not murder and to not commit adultery. No doubt, Jesus' listeners had done the same. So it's there that Jesus will begin His examination of the nature of true righteousness, with the intent not to condemn us, but to set us free.

DAY 1

Read Matthew 5:1–7:29 on pages 138-144.

As you read, underline every occurrence of the phrases "you have heard that it was said" and "it was said" with an orange pencil or marker.

1. To whom do you think Jesus is referring with this phrase? Who "said" what had been heard? Check one.

   ☐ God

   ☐ the prophets

   ☐ the teachers of the Law

Now underline every occurrence of the phrases "But I say to you," "Truly, I say to you," and "I tell you" with a purple pencil or marker.

2. Why do you think Jesus uses these phrases repeatedly?

   _____

   _____

   _____

3. Why might they cause offense to His hearers?

   _____

   _____

   _____

DAY 2

You have heard that it was said to those of old,
"You shall not murder."

MATTHEW 5:21

Read Exodus 20:13. Compare it to Matthew 5:21-26.

1. According to Matthew 5:21, what had the people heard? Had they been taught wrongly?

2. How does Jesus respond? Does He contradict what they had heard?

3. Matthew 5:22 gives three more things for which people would be held accountable. List them below:

4. Read Ephesians 4:26. Do you think it is a sin to be angry? What is the difference between sinful anger and "unsinful" anger?

_____

_____

Give an example of each.

Sinful anger: _____

_____

Unsinful anger: _____

_____

5. Can you think of a story in Scripture that would prove whether or not it is always a sin to be angry? Share it here.

_____

_____

6. Re-read Matthew 5:21-22 in the NIV. _Raca_ is the Aramaic word for empty-headed or stupid. The word _fool_ means morally worthless. Both are expressions of contempt, but _fool_ is assigned greater punishment than _raca_. Why do you think this is the case?

_____

_____

7. Look up the terms *anger* and *contempt* in your dictionary. Write a brief definition for each.

Anger: _____

_____

Contempt: _____

_____

8. What is the difference between these two emotions? How are they related?

_____

_____

9. What relationship between anger, contempt, and murder do you think Jesus is pointing out in this passage?

_____

_____

10. Jesus specifically links anger to sinful speech. How has your own anger resulted in sinful speech? List specific forms of speech your anger has taken.

_____

_____

Ask God to help you deal with your anger before your words can harmfully express it.

DAY 3

²³ So if you are offering your gift at the altar and there remember that your brother has something against you, ²⁴ leave your gift there before the altar and go. First be reconciled to your brother, and then come and offer your gift. ²⁵ Come to terms quickly with your accuser while you are going with him to court, lest your accuser hand you over to the judge, and the judge to the guard, and you be put in prison. ²⁶ Truly, I say to you, you will never get out until you have paid the last penny.

MATTHEW 5:23-26

1. In Matthew 5:23-26, what does Jesus want to teach us about fractured relationships?

2. When we offend someone, why is it important to go to that person and deal with the offense immediately?

3. How does unreconciled anger affect our ability to worship God (see Matt. 5:24)?

4. Can you think of someone toward whom you harbor anger or contempt? Consider how your anger has affected your relationship with that person:

How has it affected the other person?

How has it affected you?

What sinful actions have resulted from your anger?

5. Why do you think we tend to hold onto our anger rather than letting it go?

6. Pray and ask God to show you how to reconcile the relationship you've been reflecting on. Write down any ideas that come to mind.

DAY 4

You have heard that it was said,

"You shall not commit adultery."

MATTHEW 5:27

Read Exodus 20:14 and Matthew 5:27-30.

1. According to Matthew 5:27, what had the people heard? Had they been taught wrongly?

2. How does Jesus respond? Does He contradict what they had heard?

3. Is Jesus' discussion of anger and contempt in any way related to His discussion of adultery? Explain your answer.

4. In Matthew 5:29-30, does Jesus set forth a course of action to be followed literally? Why or why not? What point do you think He wants to make?

5. Match the following reference to its main thought:

Mark 8:34   Put to death the misdeeds of the body

Romans 8:12-14   Put to death immorality, impurity, lust, evil desires, greed

Galatians 5:24-25   Deny yourself and take up your cross

Colossians 3:1-5   Crucify the sinful nature's passions and desires

6. How do these verses shed light on Jesus' words about tearing out eyes and cutting off hands?

_____

_____

7. What are some examples of ways you can crucify the flesh daily? In other words, in what areas of your life do you need to figuratively tear out an eye or cut off a hand?

_____

_____

DAY 5

You have heard that it was said,
"You shall not commit adultery."
MATTHEW 5:27

Read Job 31:1-12 in the NIV.

1. What type of covenant did Job make?

"I have made a covenant _____ _____ _____ not to

_____ _____ at a_____ _____ "
(Job 31:1, NIV).

2. List below the "ifs" and "thens" of Job's statement.

IF	THEN

3. How seriously did Job take the issue of adultery?

4. Why do you think adultery is not taken seriously today?

5. On the issues of murder and adultery, how does Jesus challenge a casual view of what it means to be righteous? Paraphrase His views on the two topics:

    Murder:

    Adultery:

6. Have you been casual in your approach to the sins of murder and adultery? How can you take them more seriously? Write some specific thoughts.

WRAP-UP

What impacted you most in this week's passage from the Sermon on the Mount? What are the words of Jesus on dealing with anger, murder, and adultery asking of you personally?

GROUP DISCUSSION

INTRODUCTORY QUESTION: What is the best part of your weekend?

1. **REFLECT:** When is anger not a sin? When is it sinful?

   APPLY: [Day 2, question 10] Jesus specifically links anger to sinful speech. How has your own anger resulted in sinful speech? List specific forms of speech your anger has taken.

2. **REFLECT:** [Day 3, question 1] In Matthew 5:23-26, what does Jesus want to teach us about fractured relationships?

   APPLY: What should we do if the person with whom we want to reconcile has no desire to do so? What if the person we need to reconcile with is no longer living?

3. **REFLECT:** [Day 4, question 4] In Matthew 5:29-30, does Jesus set forth a course of action to be followed literally? Why or why not? What point do you think He wants to make?

   APPLY: [Day 4, question 7] What are some examples of ways you can crucify the flesh daily? In other words, in what areas of your life do you need to figuratively tear out an eye or cut off a hand?

4. **REFLECT:** On the issues of murder and adultery, how does Jesus challenge a casual view of what it means to be righteous?

   APPLY: [Day 5, question 6] Have you been casual in your approach to the sins of murder and adultery? How can you take them more seriously?

WRAP-UP: What impacted you most in this week's passage from the Sermon on the Mount? What are the words of Jesus on dealing with anger, murder, and adultery asking of you personally?

VIDEO

Watch the teaching video for Week 4. Use the space below to take notes.

NOTES

[Handwritten notes:]

anger to contempt

- Anger is our natural response to having our will violated.

Un resolved anger interferes with our worship of a almighty God.

Those who love the Lord flee from Sin

Lust is wanting something that is not yours

We walk in forgiveness Toward others because of Christ's example.

We walk in forgiveness Toward others because of Christ example

I give mercy instead of justice because it has been given to me

After the video concludes, close your study in prayer. Ask God to show you where you have wanted to "walk the line" rather than flee from sin with regard to anger and lust. Ask Him to teach you to deal ruthlessly with sin. Praise Him that because of the cross He is no longer angry with us. Thank Him for His faithfulness to you and for His forgiveness of all your sins of the past, present, and future.

YOU HAVE HEARD THAT

IT WAS SAID

PART 2

Last week Jesus began answering the question, "What does the righteousness of a follower of Christ look like?" He challenged us to a deeper obedience to the Law, one in which both our actions and our motives are pure. We considered the difference between asking, "How far is too far?" and asking, "How can I flee from sin?"

Having examined the root sins behind murder and adultery, Jesus now turns His attention to three further areas of the Law that had been taught in harmful ways: divorce, oaths, and restitution. Much of what He has to say is hard to hear, particularly to our modern ears. This particular section of the Sermon on the Mount has been the source of much controversy. Is a divorced woman who remarries an adulteress? Is it a sin to swear an oath in a court of law or to say the Pledge of Allegiance? Should we allow our enemies to take advantage of us to our harm? It would seem that we, too, "have heard that it was said."

I can't think of a better reason to look closely at these verses in context to see what Jesus would have us learn. Perhaps His original hearers were not the only ones who needed clarification on the true nature of righteousness.

DAY 1

Read Matthew 5:1–7:29 on pages 138-144.

1. Next to each section of the sermon we have studied thus far, write a phrase that summarizes its message:

Matthew 5:1-12:

_____

Matthew 5:13-16: *we are the light of the world*

_____

Matthew 5:17-20:

_____

Matthew 5:21-26: *What we think*

_____

Matthew 5:27-30: *Get rid of what is causing the sin*

_____

Now transfer your summary statements to the margin of your copy of the text on pages 138-139, writing them next to the section they summarize.

2. How does what Jesus talked about in Matthew 5:21-30 flow logically into His discussion in Matthew 5:31-48?

_____

_____

DAY 2

It was also said "Whoever divorces his wife,
let him give her a certificate of divorce."
MATTHEW 5:31

Divorce is a painful and personal topic for many of us. It's also a difficult topic to study in Scripture. As you read today, pray and ask God to help you set aside the lens of your own experience or of past teaching you have heard. Ask Him to help you read carefully for the original meaning and intent of the passages we will study. Ask Him to remind you of His infinite goodness in all He commands.

Read Deuteronomy 24:1-4 and Matthew 5:31-32.

1. According to Matthew 5:31, what had the people heard? Had they been taught wrongly?

2. How does Jesus respond? Does He contradict what they had heard?

Now read Matthew 19:3-9. Jesus spoke further here on the topic of marriage and remarriage.

3. The Pharisees wanted to test Jesus with a question about divorce. How does Jesus' reply in Matthew 19:4-6 contrast with their question?

4. How do Jesus' words in Matthew 19:3-9 shed further light on His meaning in Matthew 5:31-32? Is Jesus forbidding divorce or second marriages? (This is a tough one, so give your best answer based on the text. We'll discuss this further in the video teaching time.)

5. How does Jesus' teaching on divorce in Matthew 5:31-32 and 19:3-9 stand in contrast to the way people view marriage and divorce today?

6. If divorce has impacted your life directly, in what way are Jesus' words painful to hear?

How are His words comforting?

DAY 3

Again you have heard that it was said to those of old,
"You shall not swear falsely."
MATTHEW 5:33

1. Read the following passages and note what you learn about oath-taking in the Old Testament:

   Exodus 20:7: _____

   Leviticus 19:11-12: _____

   Numbers 30:1-2: _____

   Deuteronomy 23:21-23: _____

2. Read Matthew 5:33-37. According to verse 33, what had the people heard? Had they been taught wrongly?

   _____

   _____

3. How does Jesus respond? Does He contradict what they had heard?

   _____

   _____

SERMON ON THE MOUNT

4. Some people have taken Jesus' words to mean that a Christian should never take an oath of any kind (Pledge of Allegiance, oath of office, etc.). How would you respond to this interpretation?

5. Restate in your own words what you think Jesus means by, "Let what you say be simply 'Yes' or 'No'; anything more than this comes from evil" (Matt. 5:37).

6. How has our culture relaxed this teaching?

7. Have you ever verbally committed to do something you later failed to do? Think of a time that you have broken your word. Why do you think it is particularly important for Christ followers to be as good as their word?

DAY 4

> *You have heard that it was said,*
> *"An eye for an eye and a tooth for a tooth."*
> **MATTHEW 5:38**

Read Leviticus 24:20 and Matthew 5:38-42.

1. According to Matthew 5:38, what had the people heard? Had they been taught wrongly?

2. How does Jesus respond? Does He contradict what they had heard?

Carefully read Deuteronomy 19:16-21.

3. Based on the context, to whom was the instruction "an eye for an eye" given (19:21)? Check one:

    ☐ the accuser

    ☐ the accused

    ☐ the judges

4. Based on your answer to the previous question, how do you think the teachers of the Law were wrongly applying the principle of "an eye for an eye"?

5. What do you think was the positive intent of this law as given in the Old Testament? How could it protect the accused as well as the accuser?

6. Which of the Beatitudes seems to fit best with Jesus' description of responding to mistreatment (Matt. 5:39-42)? Explain your answer.

7. Why do you think believers struggle to follow the instruction Jesus gives about turning the other cheek or going the extra mile?

8. What is accomplished by turning the other cheek? What is risked?

9. Why do you think believers struggle to follow Jesus' instruction to, "Give to the one who begs from you, and do not refuse the one who would borrow from you" (5:42)?

10. What types of wrong thinking prevent us from being faithful to carry out these instructions?

11. Is there someone toward whom you are afraid or unwilling to practice non-retaliation? How would Jesus instruct you to respond to that person's insults or persecution?

12. Is there someone toward whom you are reluctant to practice giving or lending? How would Jesus instruct you to loosen your grip on your stuff?

DAY 5

You have heard that it was said,

"You shall love your neighbor and hate your enemy."

MATTHEW 5:43

Read Leviticus 19:18 and Matthew 5:43-48.

1. According to Matthew 5:43, what had the people heard? Had they been taught wrongly? (Be careful!)

2. How does Jesus respond? Does He contradict what they had heard?

3. Summarize what Jesus is saying in Matthew 5:44-47.

4. What do you think it means to "be perfect, as your heavenly Father is perfect" (5:48)?

5. Look through Matthew 5:43-47 for specific "perfections" of God that are mentioned. How do they instruct us in how we should treat those around us?

6. Jesus, the Son of His Father in heaven, loved His enemies and prayed for those who persecuted Him (see Matt. 5:44-45). Did Jesus choose His enemies? In light of this, how would you define an "enemy"?

7. Do you have enemies? How can you follow Christ's example in dealing with them?

8. Think back to the Beatitudes. Which character trait do you think is most necessary to fulfill the command to love those who persecute you? Why?

Ask God to help you cultivate that character trait. Ask Him to help you in specific relationships.

WRAP-UP

What impacted you most in this week's passage from the Sermon on the Mount? What are the words of Jesus on marriage, pure speech, non-retribution, and loving enemies asking of you personally?

GROUP DISCUSSION

INTRODUCTORY QUESTION: What is your favorite season of the year? Why is it your favorite?

1. **REFLECT:** [Day 2, question 5] How does Jesus' teaching on divorce in Matthew 5:31-32 and 19:3-9 stand in contrast to the way people view marriage and divorce today?

   APPLY: How has Jesus' teaching on divorce impacted your own view of marriage?

2. **REFLECT:** [Day 3, question 5] Restate in your own words what you think Jesus means by, "Let what you say be simply 'Yes' or 'No'; anything more than this comes from evil" (Matt. 5:37).

   APPLY: What steps can you take to align your words with your commitments? How can you begin to stop over-promising and/or under-delivering?

3. **REFLECT:** [Day 4, question 6] Which of the Beatitudes seems to fit best with Jesus' description of responding to mistreatment (Matt. 5:39-42)? Explain your answer.

   APPLY: [Day 4, questions 11-12] Is there someone toward whom you are afraid or unwilling to practice non-retaliation? How would Jesus instruct you to respond to that person's insults or persecution? Is there someone toward whom you are reluctant to practice giving or lending? How would Jesus instruct you to loosen your grip on your stuff?

4. **REFLECT:** [Day 5, question 3] Summarize what Jesus is saying in Matthew 5:44-47.

   APPLY: [Day 5, question 7] Do you have enemies? How can you follow Christ's example in dealing with them?

WRAP-UP: What impacted you most in this week's passage from the Sermon on the Mount? What are the words of Jesus on marriage, pure speech, non-retribution, and loving enemies asking of you personally?

VIDEO

Watch the teaching video for Week 5. Use the space below to take notes.

NOTES

After the video concludes, close your study in prayer. Ask God to help you culti-vate and maintain a high view of marriage. Ask Him to draw you into a deeper obedience with regard to your words and your treatment of others. Praise God that His "yes" is always "yes" and His "no" is always "no." Thank Him that He treats us not as we deserve, but with a preferential love—a love that turned its cheek and went the extra mile.

SECRET

RIGHTEOUSNESS

It's probably safe to say that each of us grapples with the sin of approval seeking, of desiring to win the praise and attention of others. We even use the outwardly righteous practices of our faith to focus attention on ourselves. In Matthew 6:1-18, Jesus will address this tendency head-on.

For the past two weeks of our study, Jesus has focused on teaching a deeper obedience to the "don'ts"—don't murder, don't commit adultery, and so on. This week He begins teaching a deeper obedience to the "dos"—do give to the needy, do pray, do fast. Our focus will shift from considering what it truly means to do the wrong thing to what it truly means to do the right thing.

Just as we are not righteous simply by avoiding forbidden actions, we are not righteous simply by practicing commanded actions. Our motives must match our outward obedience. Jesus will continue to faithfully pry from His listeners' grip the desire to live a "bare minimum" faith—one in which we seek to invest as little effort as possible to enjoy as many benefits as possible as followers of Christ. Instead He will point us to an abundant faith, one that breathes righteousness into even the "secret" moments of our lives.

DAY 1

Read Matthew 5:1–7:29 on pages 138-144.

As you read, circle each occurrence of the phrase "your Father" with a brown pencil or marker.

1. How many times does this phrase occur? _____

2. Choose a passage of the sermon that has become very familiar to you after repeated reading and study. Write it on a note card and spend some time committing it to memory.

3. Now go back and read Matthew 6:1-18. Think of a movie or television show in which pastors or Christians are portrayed in a negative light. What negative stereotypes or behaviors are associated with these portrayals?

    _____

    _____

    Why do you think these negative perceptions exist?

    _____

    _____

4. Compare Matthew 6:1 to 5:16. Do you see a contradiction in Jesus' words? Why or why not?

    _____

    _____

DAY 2

1. In Matthew 6, Jesus begins a discussion of acts of righteousness. Look back at this chapter and fill in the chart.

Act of Righteousness	What the Hypocrite Does	His Reward	What the Righteous Man Does	His Reward
Matthew 6:2-4				
Matthew 6:5-15				
Matthew 6:16-18				

> ² When you give to the needy, sound no trumpet before you, as the hypocrites do in the synagogues and in the streets, that they may be praised by others. Truly, I say to you, they have received their reward. ³ But when you give to the needy, do not let your left hand know what your right hand is doing, ⁴ so that your giving may be in secret. And your Father who sees in secret will reward you.
>
> **MATTHEW 6:2-4**

2. According to verse 2, what was wrong with the way the hypocrites were giving?

3. What do you think Jesus means by, "When you give to the needy, do not let your left hand know what your right hand is doing" (6:3)?

Why is this approach to giving important (6:2,4)?

4. What does a modern-day hypocritical giver look like? List some thoughts or examples.

5. Should all giving be done in secret? Why or why not?

6. In what ways are you tempted to give hypocritically? What kinds of giving appeal to your pride?

7. How could you give to that same recipient in a God-honoring way?

DAY 3

⁵ And when you pray, you must not be like the hypocrites. For they love to stand and pray in the synagogues and at the street corners, that they may be seen by others. Truly, I say to you, they have received their reward. ⁶ But when you pray, go into your room and shut the door and pray to your Father who is in secret. And your Father who sees in secret will reward you.

⁷And when you pray, do not heap up empty phrases as the Gentiles do, for they think that they will be heard for their many words. ⁸ Do not be like them, for your Father knows what you need before you ask him.

MATTHEW 6:5-8

1. If your prayers were written down like those in the Psalms, what would those who read them learn about your concept of God?

2. According to Matthew 6:5, what was wrong with the prayers of the hypocrites?

Can a prayer request ever be used in a hypocritical way? Give an example.

3. Read Matthew 26:39-44. What is the difference between the type of prayer described in Matthew 6:7 and the persistent prayer of Jesus?

4. How are we guilty of "heap[ing] up empty phrases" when we pray?

5. What do the following verses teach us about prayer?

John 9:31:

John 15:7:

If our Father knows what we need before we ask Him, why should we pray?

6. What aspect of the prayer of the hypocrite is most convicting to you? Would changing your words correct the problem?

7. What makes our prayers acceptable to God?

DAY 4

> [16]And when you fast, do not look gloomy like the hypocrites, for they disfigure their faces that their fasting may be seen by others. Truly, I say to you, they have received their reward. [17] But when you fast, anoint your head and wash your face, [18] that your fasting may not be seen by others but by your Father who is in secret. And your Father who sees in secret will reward you.

MATTHEW 6:16-18

1. What was the problem with the way the hypocrites of Jesus' day were fasting?

_____

_____

Fasting was practiced in many ways and for many reasons. A fast could be partial (see Dan. 10:2-3) or total (see Matt. 4:1-2), voluntary (see Dan. 9:3) or involuntary (see Dan. 6:18). The key concept in fasting was always the removal of something from everyday life in order to focus on God. For example, in Daniel 10, each time Daniel refused delicacies, meat, or wine during his fast, he was reminded of his position before God.

Read Isaiah 58:1-12.

2. According to verses 1-4, why were the Israelites fasting?

_____

_____

3. Were they walking in righteousness before God? Explain.

_____

_____

4. In verse 5 we learn what the people were doing when they fasted. List some of these things.

_____

_____

_____

5. According to verses 6-7, what kind of fast had God chosen?

_____

_____

6. In Isaiah 58:8-12, note each occurrence of "if" and "then." What are the end results of a godly fast?

_____

_____

_____

7. Why do you think fasting is not widely practiced today? Do you think it should be?

_____

_____

If so, what are some ways modern Christians can fast?

_____

_____

8. How do modern-day hypocrites abuse the discipline of fasting to receive glory for themselves rather than for God?

_____

_____

9. Note that Jesus says, "*when* you fast" (Matt. 6:16, emphasis mine). When do you fast? Pray and ask God to show you if there is something He would have you fast from that you might grow closer to Him. Write down some possible things from which you could fast.

_____

_____

_____

_____

DAY 5

¹⁴For if you forgive others their trespasses, your heavenly Father will also forgive you, ¹⁵ but if you do not forgive others their trespasses, neither will your Father forgive your trespasses.

MATTHEW 6:14-15

1. Each of the following terms represent a key element in the Lord's Prayer. Look up each term in a dictionary and write a brief definition.

Confession: _____

Submission: _____

Deliverance: _____

Petition: _____

Worship: _____

Allegiance: _____

2. Now, write each term beside the section of the Lord's Prayer to which you think it belongs. (Note them also in your copy of the text on page 141.)

"Our Father in heaven,
   hallowed be your name."

"Your kingdom come."

"Your will be done on
   earth as it is in heaven."

"Give us this day our
   daily bread."

"Forgive us our debts, as we also
   have forgiven our debtors."

"And lead us not into temptation,
   but deliver us from evil."

3. Read Psalm 96. What does this psalm teach us about the element of *worship* in prayer?

4. Read 1 John 5:14-15. What do these verses teach us about the element of *submission* in prayer?

5. Read James 1:2-3,13-15. How do these verses shape our interpretation of "Lead us not into temptation, but deliver us from evil"?

6. Matthew 6:14-15 reiterates one thought contained in the Lord's Prayer. Which one? Why do you think Jesus reiterates that particular idea?

Read 1 Chronicles 4:9-10. Not long ago, this particular Old Testament prayer became enormously popular among Christians. Believers were encouraged to pray it repeatedly for a 30-day period and watch how God worked in their lives.

7. How many of the six key elements found in the Lord's Prayer are contained in the prayer of 1 Chronicles 4:9-10? Which ones can you identify?

8. What do you think the enormous popularity of this prayer reflects about Christian culture today?

9. The Lord's Prayer has been given to us as a model of how to pray. Which of the six key elements of the Lord's Prayer needs more emphasis in your prayers?

_____

_____

WRAP-UP

What impacted you most in this week's passage from the Sermon on the Mount? What are the words of Jesus on giving, praying, and fasting asking of you personally?

_____

_____

GROUP DISCUSSION

INTRODUCTORY QUESTION: What snack food do you find irresistible? What is your "food kryptonite"?

1. **REFLECT:** [Day 2, question 3] What do you think Jesus means by, "When you give to the needy, do not let your left hand know what your right hand is doing" (6:3)?

   APPLY: What are some ways we can practice our giving without being hypocrites?

2. **REFLECT:** [Day 3, question 2] According to Matthew 6:5, what was wrong with the prayers of the hypocrites?

   APPLY: How are you tempted toward hypocrisy in your own prayers? What situations or circumstances make genuine prayer hardest for you?

3. **REFLECT:** [Day 4, question 6] According to Isaiah 58:8-12, what are the end results of a godly fast?

   APPLY: [Day 4, question 7] Why do you think fasting is not widely practiced today? Do you think it should be? If so, what are some ways modern Christians can fast?

4. **REFLECT:** [Day 5, questions 7-8] How many of the six key elements found in the Lord's Prayer are contained in the prayer of 1 Chronicles 4:9-10? What do you think the enormous popularity of this prayer reflects about Christian culture today?

   APPLY: [Day 5, question 9] The Lord's Prayer has been given to us as a model of how to pray. Which of the six key elements of the Lord's Prayer needs more emphasis in your own prayers?

WRAP-UP: What impacted you most in this week's passage from the Sermon on the Mount? What are the words of Jesus on giving, praying, and fasting asking of you personally?

VIDEO

Watch the teaching video for Week 6. Use the space below to take notes.

NOTES

After the video concludes, close your study in prayer. Praise God that He is worthy of our obedience, both public and private. Ask Him to help you develop the habits of secret praying, giving, and fasting. Ask Him for the wisdom to know when to show and when to hide your acts of obedience. Thank God that He does not merely command us to pray, but that He instructs us how. Thank Him that He sees you in the secret place.

WHERE YOUR TREASURE

IS

Last week Jesus addressed the way we give, pray, and fast—three righteous acts intended to turn our attention heavenward. Because we are lovers of self, we can turn even that which should humble us into that which becomes a source of pride. We can perform our acts of righteousness not to bring glory to God, but to ourselves. We were reminded that God is a God who sees us in the secret place, a truth that is both a caution and a beautiful assurance. And we were given a pattern for prayer to help us orient our hearts humbly toward our Father in heaven.

This week Jesus turns our attention earthward , challenging us to think differently about how we relate to the money, possessions, and other earthly treasures that consume our time and energy. Not surprisingly, Jesus will address the worry and anxiety inevitably associated with storing up treasures on earth. Most of us battle worry, either during a stressful season of life or as a constant nagging companion lurking in the back of our consciousness. Jesus intends to free us from the misconception that worry and anxiety are normal in the life of a disciple, and to gently direct us to a better way: trusting in an infinitely good Father who knows and supplies perfectly the needs of His children.

DAY 1

Read Matthew 5:1–7:29 on pages 138-144.

1. As you read, circle each occurrence of the words "reward" or "treasure" with a yellow pencil or marker. Based on how this concept is presented throughout the sermon, what kind of reward or treasure should we set our hope on?

2. Take 15 minutes to practice memorizing the passage you chose last week.

Now read Matthew 6:19-34.

3. How does this week's passage follow logically on the heels of the passage we focused on in Week 6 (see Matt. 6:1-18)?

4. Summarize the main idea of Matthew 6:19-24.

WHERE YOUR TREASURE IS

5. Summarize the main idea of Matthew 6:25-34.

Now transfer your summary statements to the margin of your copy of the text on pages 142-143, writing them next to the section they summarize.

DAY 2

> ¹⁹ Do not lay up for yourselves treasures on earth, where moth and rust destroy and where thieves break in and steal, ²⁰ but lay up for yourselves treasures in heaven, where neither moth nor rust destroys and where thieves do not break in and steal. ²¹ For where your treasure is, there your heart will be also.
>
> **MATTHEW 6:19-21**

1. Why do you think Jesus says we should lay up heavenly treasures instead of earthly ones?

How, practically, can we do this? List some thoughts below.

2. Is Jesus teaching that it is wrong for the Christian to possess personal property, savings, or insurance policies? Why or why not?

Read Proverbs 30:1-9.

3. What two things did Agur request of God with regard to riches?

4. Compare Proverbs 30:8 in the ESV and NIV. What did Agur ask God to give him "only" (NIV)?

How might this add to your understanding (and use) of the Lord's Prayer?

Read Revelation 3:14-22.

5. What does verse 17 tell us about the source of the apathy of the Laodiceans?

6. What three conditions listed in verse 17 does verse 18 counsel them to remedy by seeking God?

7. Can you find each of these three conditions addressed in Matthew 6:19-34? Go back to your responses in question 6 and note the relevant verse(s) next to each condition.

8. Read 2 Peter 3:10-14. What do these verses teach us about material versus spiritual possessions?

How does verse 11 suggest that we lay up treasures in heaven?

9. What do you think is meant by the phrase, "Where your treasure is, there your heart will be also" (Matt. 6:21)?

Restate Matthew 6:21 in your own words.

_____

_____

10. Now read Psalm 24:1-2 in the ESV and the NIV. How can you live in the light of these verses so that your heart and treasure are where they should be?

_____

_____

DAY 3

> ²² *The eye is the lamp of the body. So, if your eye is healthy, your whole body will be full of light,* ²³ *but if your eye is bad, your whole body will be full of darkness. If then the light in you is darkness, how great is the darkness!*
> ²⁴ *No one can serve two masters, for either he will hate the one and love the other, or he will be devoted to the one and despise the other. You cannot serve God and money.*
>
> **MATTHEW 6:22-24**

1. In Week 4 we studied a passage in Job in which Job had made a special covenant. Note Job's words in Job 31:1:

"I have made a covenant _____ _____ _____."

What role do you think the eyes play in the committing of sin?

_____

_____

2. Read Genesis 3:1-6. What process does Eve go through in verse 6?

    1. She _____ the apple.

    2. She _____desired_____ the apple.

    3. She _____ the apple.

    4. She _____ the apple.

    5. She _____ the apple to Adam.

3. When Joshua is commanded to take the city to Jericho, God gives specific instructions about what to do with the spoils (see Josh. 6:18-19; 7:1). Achan, one of his commanders, disobeys these instructions. Read Joshua 7:19-25 and note the similarities between Achan's story and Eve's story.

    _____

    _____

4. Read 2 Samuel 11:1-5,14,26-27. What similarities can you find between David's story and those you have just studied?

    _____

    _____

5. Read the following passages and note what each teaches about our eyes.

2 Corinthians 4:18:

_____

_____

Hebrews 12:2:

_____

_____

1 John 2:15-17:

_____

_____

6. How does 1 John 2:15-17 relate to Matthew 6:24?

_____

_____

7. Restate Matthew 6:22-23 in your own words.

_____

_____

8. In Matthew 6:24, Jesus warns that you cannot serve two masters. Many people hold down two jobs to support a family. In effect, they serve two masters. How is what Jesus is saying different from this scenario (i.e. what does the term "master" mean to Him)?

9. What worldly "master" is fighting for your loyalties in your daily life? On what master have you "fixed your eyes"? Write it below. Pray and ask God to help you see and serve Him rather than temporal pleasures or pursuits.

DAY 4

Therefore I tell you, do not be anxious about your life …
MATTHEW 6:25

Read Matthew 6:25-30.

1. What two images from nature does Jesus use to illustrate why we should not be anxious for anything?

What is His point in choosing these two images?

2. What do you think food and clothing represent in this passage? Check the paraphrase you think fits most closely with Jesus' meaning in 6:28.

    ☐ Do not worry about which foods to eat and which clothes to wear.

    ☐ Do not worry about having enough food to eat or enough clothes to wear.

    Do we usually spend our time worrying about basic needs or about "extras"? Explain your response.

3. Read Matthew 6:25-30. How will the treasures and masters we choose in verses 19-24 impact our ability to live lives free from worry?

4. In verse 30, Jesus refers to His listeners as "O you of little faith." What relationship is Jesus indicating exists between worry and faith?

5. Does relying solely on God's provision relieve us of the responsibility of working? Read 2 Thessalonians 3:6-15. How does Paul answer this question?

6. What things consume the most time and energy in your life? Write them below. We will revisit your answer on Day 5.

_____

_____

7. What are you most anxious about? List those things here.

_____

_____

Read 1 Peter 5:6-7. How can you apply these verses to your list of anxieties?

_____

_____

Pray and ask God to teach you the humility of casting your anxieties on Him.

DAY 5

> [31] *Therefore do not be anxious, saying, "What shall we eat?" or "What shall we drink?" or "What shall we wear?"* [32] *For the Gentiles seek after all these things, and your heavenly Father knows that you need them all.* [33] *But seek first the kingdom of God and his righteousness, and all these things will be added to you.*
>
> [34] *Therefore do not be anxious about tomorrow, for tomorrow will be anxious for itself. Sufficient for the day is its own trouble.*
>
> **MATTHEW 6:31-34**

1. Compare Matthew 6:31-34 in the ESV and the NIV. Give examples of how people today "run after all these things" (v. 32, NIV) that Jesus mentions.

2. Read Matthew 25:41-45. God promises to feed and clothe His children, but many today are in need of these things. Why might this be the case?

3. What does it mean to seek first His kingdom?

To seek first His righteousness?

4. List below your top three priorities in sentence form:

5. In yesterday's lesson we asked ourselves what things consume the most time
    and energy in our lives. Does your list of top priorities reflect where your time
    and energy are spent? Explain.

Pray and ask God to help your priorities and your efforts align.

WRAP-UP

What impacted you most in this week's passage from the Sermon on the
Mount? What are the words of Jesus regarding treasures and worry asking
of you personally?

GROUP DISCUSSION

INTRODUCTORY QUESTION: Describe the best gift you have received and why it is your favorite.

1. **REFLECT:** Look back over questions 4 and 5 on Day 1. Summarize the main ideas of Matthew 6:19-34.

   APPLY: [Day 2, question 9] What do you think is meant by the phrase, "Where your treasure is, there your heart will be also" (Matt. 6:21)?

2. **REFLECT:** Look back over questions 2, 3, and 4 on Day 3. When you "see" something that tempts you, what can you do to stop the process of sin seen in these Scripture passages? In other words, what should Eve, Achan, and David have done differently?

   APPLY: What does Jesus mean by the word "master" in 6:24? [Day 3, question 9] What worldly "master" is fighting for your loyalties in your daily life? On what master have you "fixed your eyes"?

3. **REFLECT:** [Day 4, question 3] How will the treasures and masters we choose in 6:19-24 impact our ability to live lives free from worry?

   APPLY: [Day 4, question 7] What are you most anxious about? How can you apply 1 Peter 5:6-7 to your list of anxieties?

4. **REFLECT:** [Day 5, question 3] What does it mean to seek first His kingdom? His righteousness?

   APPLY: [Day 5, question 1] Give examples of how people today "run after all these things" (Matt. 6:32, NIV) that Jesus mentions.

WRAP-UP: What impacted you most in this week's passage from the Sermon on the Mount? What are the words of Jesus regarding treasures and worry asking of you personally?

VIDEO

Watch the teaching video for Week 7. Use the space below to take notes.

NOTES

After the video concludes, close your study in prayer. Praise God that by His grace you can invest now in things of eternal significance. Ask Him to help you have one treasure, one vision, one master. Confess your worries and anxieties as unbelief. Thank Him that He knows your needs and takes pleasure in meeting them.

DO

UNTO OTHERS

Last week we learned that there were two places we can store up treasure: in heaven or on earth. We learned that there are two masters we have to choose between: God or self. And we learned that there are two directions we can fix our gaze: on what is good or on what is evil. Jesus took great care to instruct us on choosing the better thing. Connecting worry to the pursuit of the wrong treasure, master, and vision, He admonished us not to worry about ourselves, what we would eat, drink, or wear. These matters, He assured, can be trusted to our good Father in heaven.

This week we will consider the way we view the sin of others, as well as our own sin. "Judge not, that you be not judged" (Matt. 7:1) is one of those verses everyone, Christian or non-Christian, likes to quote freely. But do we quote it in a way that is faithful to the teaching of Jesus or in a way that serves our own interests? And what about asking, seeking, and knocking? Does Jesus mean for us to understand that God needs to be convinced of our earnestness when we pray? And what about "Do to others what you would have them do to you" (Matt. 7:12, NIV)? Is the Golden Rule a command to treat others fairly, or is it perhaps something more than that? As He has done thus far in the Sermon on the Mount, Jesus will ask of us a deeper obedience than we might otherwise offer. May God give us ears to hear His words afresh this week.

DAY 1

Read Matthew 5:1–7:29 on pages 138-144.

1. Take 15 minutes to work on committing to memory the passage you chose. If you have already memorized your chosen passage, ask God to show you other passages you could begin to learn.

2. Look back at Day 1 of week 7 (pp. 92-93). Recopy your summary statements for the following passages.

   Matthew 6:19-24:

   _____

   _____

   Matthew 6:25-34:

   _____

   _____

   Now read Matthew 7:1-12.

3. As you read, mark every direct command in this section of the text. Mark each "do" with a green wavy underline. Mark each "don't" with a red jagged underline. If you love annotating, feel free to do this for the entire Sermon on the Mount for commands both implied and stated.

4. How does this week's passage follow logically on the heels of Matthew 6:19-34?

   _____

   _____

DAY 2

¹ Judge not, that you be not judged. ² For with the judgment you pronounce you will be judged, and with the measure you use it will be measured to you. ³ Why do you see the speck that is in your brother's eye, but do not notice the log that is in your own eye? ⁴ Or how can you say to your brother, "Let me take the speck out of your eye," when there is the log in your own eye? ⁵ You hypocrite, first take the log out of your own eye, and then you will see clearly to take the speck out of your brother's eye.

MATTHEW 7:1-5

1. Look back through the Sermon on the Mount and list below passages that express a similar thought to that of Matthew 7:1-2.

2. In Matthew 7:3-5, Jesus uses a colorful illustration to teach a basic truth about human nature. What are the similarities and differences between a speck of sawdust and a log? What does each represent? Fill in the chart below.

	SPECK OF SAWDUST	LOG
Same		
Different		
Meaning		

3. Consider Jesus' audience for the Sermon on the Mount. Next to each group of "listeners" below, note why you think Jesus chose this particular topic. What did He want to communicate to each group and why?

The disciples

The crowds

The scribes and Pharisees

4. In Matthew 7:4-5, whose eye was it that contained a speck of sawdust?

Why do you think Jesus uses this term?

5. Is Jesus commanding that we are never to judge others? Read the following verses and note the main thought of each:

James 5:19-20:

_____

Galatians 6:1:

_____

Based on these verses, what type of judging is Jesus warning against in Matthew 7:1-5?

_____

_____

6. Read Romans 2:1-6,21-24. How do these verses add to your understanding of Matthew 7:1-5?

_____

_____

_____

7. Upon whom are you guilty of passing judgment for a sin that is also your own? Confess your own sin to God. Ask Him to help you extend grace instead of judgment to those who offend you with similar sins to your own.

_____

_____

DAY 3

Do not give dogs what is holy, and do not throw your pearls before pigs, lest they trample them underfoot and turn to attack you.

MATTHEW 7:6

To the Jew, both dogs and pigs were considered unclean animals. The "dogs" Jesus refers to in His analogy would not have been domesticated animals, but wild and ferocious animals that scavenged and stole to survive.

Read Philippians 3:2-3,17-19.

1. Who are the "dogs" in this passage?

How would they fit the statement Jesus makes in Matthew 7:6?

Read 2 Peter 2:1-3,21-22.

2. Who are described as "dogs" and "pigs" in this chapter?

How would they fit the statement that Jesus makes in verse 6?

How are they different from the "dogs" described in Philippians 3:2-3,17-19?

_____

What type of behavior is represented in the analogy found in 2 Peter 2:22?

_____

_____

3. If we are to "judge not" (7:1), how are we to discern who is a dog or a pig?

_____

4. What do you think are the "holy" things or "pearls" we are not to offer to "dogs" and "pigs" in Matthew 7:6?

_____

5. Read the following verses and note how they relate to Matthew 7:6.

Proverbs 23:9:

_____

Proverbs 9:7-9:

_____

2 Corinthians 2:14-16:

_____

6. Now rewrite Matthew 7:6 in your own words.

7. Have you ever been met with total rejection after sharing the gospel? How can we know whether we are dealing with pigs and dogs, or with someone who might respond to the gospel at a later time?

DAY 4

> *7 Ask, and it will be given to you; seek, and you will find; knock, and it will be opened to you. 8 For everyone who asks receives, and the one who seeks finds, and to the one who knocks it will be opened.*
>
> **MATTHEW 7:7-8**

1. What assurance does Jesus give those who ask, seek, and knock?

2. Why do you think Jesus offers this type of encouragement at this point in His discourse?

3. Based on the topics Jesus has covered thus far, what things might the disciples be moved to request with urgency and persistence?

_____

_____

4. "Ask, and it will be given to you" (7:7) could be taken to mean that God grants whatever we ask. Read the passages below and form a response to this misconception.

James 4:1-3: _____

_____

Proverbs 28:9: _____

_____

5. Note the progression in the three actions Jesus encourages. How does each action build on the idea of how to request things from God? Paraphrase the action you think each implies.

Ask: _____

_____

Seek: _____

_____

Knock: _____

_____

6. The tense of each of the three verbs indicates a continuous and ongoing action (i.e. keep asking, keep seeking, keep knocking). Why does Jesus teach that prayer requires persistence?

7. If God does not need to be encouraged, convinced, or coerced, why might He not answer a request made only once?

8. Is there something for which you have *kept* asking, *kept* seeking, and *kept* knocking? How are Jesus' words an encouragement to you?

DAY 5

> [9] *Which one of you, if his son asks him for bread, will give him a stone? [10] Of if he asks for a fish, will give him a serpent? [11] If you then, who are evil, know how to give good gifts to your children, how much more will your Father who is in heaven give good things to those who ask him!*
>
> [12] *So whatever you wish that others would do to you, do also to them, for this is the Law and the Prophets.*

MATTHEW 7:9-12

1. Read Luke 11:1-13. In this corresponding passage to Matthew 7:9-12, Jesus gives an illustration of a man going to his neighbor to ask for bread. How does this illustration expand your understanding of how God responds to our requests?

2. In Matthew 7:11, to whom is Jesus referring when He says, "If *you*, then, who are evil …"?

3. Based on Matthew 7:9-11, does God give as a parent gives to a child? Explain.

4. What is the name commonly known for Matthew 7:12?

5. The Jewish Talmud (sacred writings) commanded: "What is hateful to you, do not do unto your neighbor." Confucius commanded his followers: "Do not to others what you would not wish done to you." How does Jesus' command go beyond those of the Talmud and Confucius?

6. Compare Matthew 7:12 in the ESV and NIV. In what sense does the Golden Rule sum up the Law and the Prophets?

7. Is there someone toward whom you hesitate to demonstrate the Golden Rule? Who?

Why do you think it is so difficult to treat that particular person the way you would like to be treated?

How could you ask God to change your thinking about that person (or about yourself) to make it easier for you to treat him or her better?

WRAP-UP

What impacted you most in this week's passage from the Sermon on the Mount? What are the words of Jesus on judging, persistent requesting, and doing to others asking of you personally?

GROUP DISCUSSION

INTRODUCTORY QUESTION: What did you consider to be the most valuable thing you owned when you were a child? When you were a teenager? How about now?

1. **REFLECT:** [Day 2, questions 6] Read Romans 2:1-6,21-24. How do these verses add to your understanding of Matthew 7:1-5?

   APPLY: Which sins or categories of sins are you most likely to judge others for that you also commit?

2. **REFLECT:** [Day 3, questions 3-4] If we are to "judge not" (7:1), how are we to discern who is a dog or a pig? What do you think are the "holy" things or "pearls" we are not to offer to "dogs" and "pigs" in 7:6?

   APPLY: [Day 3, question 7] Have you ever been met with total rejection after sharing the gospel? How can we know whether we are dealing with pigs and dogs, or with someone who might respond to the gospel at a later time?

3. **REFLECT:** Read Matthew 7:7. Has your understanding of this frequently quoted verse changed as you have studied it within the context of the Sermon on the Mount? If yes, how? [Day 4, question 3] Based on the topics Jesus has covered thus far, what things might the disciples be moved to request with urgency and persistence?

   APPLY: How has studying the Sermon on the Mount as a whole influenced that for which you will ask, seek, and knock?

4. **REFLECT:** [Day 5, question 6] Compare Matthew 7:12 in the ESV and NIV. In what sense does the Golden Rule sum up the Law and the Prophets?

   APPLY: [Day 5, question 7] Is there someone toward whom you hesitate to demonstrate the Golden Rule? Why? How could you ask God to change your thinking about that person (or about yourself) to make it easier for you to treat him or her better?

WRAP-UP: What impacted you most in this week's passage from the Sermon on the Mount? What are the words of Jesus on judging, persistent requesting, and doing to others asking of you personally?

VIDEO

Watch the teaching video for Week 8. Use the space below to take notes.

NOTES

After the video concludes, close your study in prayer. Praise God that He is a "much more" Father. Ask Him to help you learn to see your own sin before you look for sin in another. Ask Him to help you trust Him as the Giver of all good things, and to increase your boldness to ask, seek, and knock for your spiritual daily bread. Thank Him that He has set His preferential love on you as a seal.

A FOUNDATION THAT ENDURES

Last week we distinguished between two kinds of "judging others."
We learned that while worldly judgment seeks to condemn and reject,
godly judgment seeks to heal and restore. We saw that we must be careful not to subject the gospel to ridicule by offering it to those who have
repeatedly and adamantly rejected it. We learned that our Heavenly Father
is a "much more" Father who does not deny His children their earnest
requests for spiritual daily bread. And we learned that the Golden Rule
asks us to show love to others not merely as they deserve, but beyond
what they deserve. It is a call to love preferentially as Christ loves us.

This week we will listen as Jesus masterfully draws His sermon to its
conclusion. Like any good teacher, Jesus ends by asking His listeners to
respond to His message. He poses a series of contrasts that will challenge
them to consider whether they resemble a citizen of heaven or a citizen
of earth: there are two kinds of gates. Which one will you choose? There
are two kinds of teachers. Which one will you listen to? There are two
kinds of servants. Which one will you be? There are two kinds of founda-
tions. On which will you build?

If ever a sermon required a response, surely it is this one. Jesus' listeners
did not know how His earthly ministry would end, but we do. If they
listened and were amazed, how much more amazed ought we be, as
those who live in light of the finished work of Christ? As you consider
what Jesus' words asked of His original hearers, consider what they
are asking of you.

DAY 1

Read Matthew 5:1–7:29 on pages 138-144 from start to finish one final time.

1. Recite aloud your passage that you committed to memory during this study.

2. After repeated readings, if you could choose one verse as the key for the Sermon on the Mount, which one would you choose? Why?

Now read Matthew 7:13-29.

3. Summarize this week's passage into two or three sections, writing your summary statements in the margin of your copy of the text on page 144 next to the section they summarize.

4. How does this week's passage follow logically on the heels of Matthew 7:1-12?

DAY 2

> *¹³ Enter by the narrow gate. For the gate is wide and the way is easy that leads to destruction, and those who enter by it are many. ¹⁴ For the gate is narrow and the way is hard that leads to life, and those who find it are few.*
>
> **MATTHEW 7:13-14**

1. In verses 13-14, Jesus describes two gates and two roads. Read these verses in the ESV and NIV.

   How are the two gates different?

   one is wide + one is narrow

   How are the two ways or roads different?

2. In what regard is the gate of Christianity small?

   In what regard is the road of Christianity narrow?

Read Luke 13:22-30.

3. In this similar passage, what is the question that is asked of Jesus?

How does Jesus answer?

4. In Luke 13:24, how might someone seek to enter the narrow gate and not be able to?

5. How have you heard people react to Jesus' statement that there is only one true gate, road, and destination?

Why do you think they react this way?

6. How narrow is the gate Jesus mentions? Look up the following verses and note what each says.

John 3:36: _____

John 10:9: _____

Acts 4:12: _____

1 Timothy 2:5: _____

1 John 5:12: _____

In what way is the truth of the narrow gate and way a warning to you?

How is it a source of assurance?

DAY 3

15 Beware of false prophets, who come to you in sheep's clothing but inwardly are ravenous wolves. 16 You will recognize them by their fruits. Are grapes gathered from thornbushes, or figs from thistles? 17 So, every healthy tree bears good fruit, but the diseased tree bears bad fruit. 18 A healthy tree cannot bear bad fruit, nor can a diseased tree bear good fruit. 19 Every tree that does not bear good fruit is cut down and thrown into the fire. 20 Thus you will recognize them by their fruits.

MATTHEW 7:15-20

1. Why do you think Jesus moves from a discussion of the wide and narrow ways to a warning about false prophets?

2. What types of sheep's clothing would false prophets wear today?

3. How is a false prophet like a ferocious wolf?

4. If we are to recognize a false prophet by his fruit, what types of fruit should we look for?

5. Read Matthew 12:33-35. What does this passage reveal as a type of fruit by which a false prophet can be identified?

6. According to Hebrews 5:11-14, how can we know if the words of a teacher are true?

7. Read 1 John 4:1-6. Are we responsible to discern between the Spirit of truth and a spirit of error? What does this passage tell us about discerning which is which?

8. Read Hebrews 4:12. What sharp implement is provided to us for the purpose of cutting down a tree that "bears bad fruit" (Matt. 7:17)?

   How skilled are you in using this tool? How can you become better at using it to discern truth from error?

DAY 4

> [21] *Not everyone who says to me, "Lord, Lord," will enter the kingdom of heaven, but the one who does the will of my Father who is in heaven.* [22] *On that day many will say to me, "Lord, Lord, did we not prophesy in your name, and cast out demons in your name, and do many mighty works in your name?"* [23] *And then will I declare to them, "I never knew you; depart from me, you workers of lawlessness."*
>
> **MATTHEW 7:21-23**

1. What do you think the statement, "Lord, Lord" is supposed to imply about the attitude of the one who speaks it?

2. The people described in verses 21-23 perform admirable deeds and speak admirable words. Why does Jesus condemn them?

3. Who has led the people astray? (Consider Matthew 7:15-20.)

4. According to Matthew 7:21, who will enter the kingdom of heaven?

_____

_____

Does this mean that salvation is earned by what we do? Why or why not?

_____

_____

5. What sort of person is described as not gaining admittance to the kingdom of heaven?

_____

_____

6. Apparently someone without saving faith can perform some amazing works in the name of Jesus. What three examples does Jesus give in Matthew 7:22?

_____

_____

_____

7. Why do you think God allows unbelievers to do remarkable things in His name? Give your best guess and then look up Philippians 1:15-18 to see Paul's thoughts on this subject.

_____

_____

8. Have you ever benefited spiritually from the ministry of someone who later turned out to be a false prophet? Describe that time.

9. How did that experience change the way you viewed people in ministry?

10. How did it change the way you viewed God?

DAY 5

> *24 Everyone then who hears these words of mine and does them will be like a wise man who built his house on the rock. 25 And the rain fell, and the floods came, and the winds blew and beat on that house, but it did not fall, because it had been founded on the rock. 26 And everyone who hears these words of mine and does not do them will be like the foolish man who built his house on the sand. 27 And the rain fell, and the floods came, and the winds blew and beat against that house, and it fell, and great was the fall of it.*
>
> **MATTHEW 7:24-27**

1. Look closely at verse 24. What two conditions must be met to be like the man who built on a rock?

2. How are the two houses in Jesus' illustration similar?

How are they different?

3. At what point would the difference(s) be revealed between the two houses?

4. Based on Matthew 7:24-27, label the picture below with what you think each part of the story about the wise man's house represents.

5. What are some examples of rain, flood, and wind that come into our lives?

Are these events always unexpected, uninvited, or undeserved? Explain.

6. Can you identify with the word picture Jesus paints in these verses? Describe a time in your life when you found Christ to be a sure foundation.

7. Matthew 7:28 says that when Jesus finished speaking, the crowds were "astonished at his teaching." Has any particular part of the Sermon on the Mount astonished you? Which one(s)? Why?

WRAP-UP

What impacted you most in this week's passage from the Sermon on the Mount? What are the words of Jesus asking of you personally?

GROUP DISCUSSION

INTRODUCTORY QUESTION: If you could build your dream home, where would it be and what would it look like?

1. **REFLECT:** Look back over questions 1 and 2 on Day 2. Specifically, how is the gate of Christianity small and the road narrow?

   APPLY: In Matthew 7:14, Jesus says, "the way is hard that leads to life." In what way(s) have you found this to be true? Have you ever crossed paths with someone who said otherwise?

2. **REFLECT:** [Day 3, question 6] According to Hebrews 5:11-14, how can we know if the words of a teacher are true?

   APPLY: Give some examples of popular false teaching among Christian circles and secular circles. How can we be careful to identify false teaching?

3. **REFLECT:** [Day 4, question 4] According to 7:21, who *will* enter the kingdom of heaven? Does this mean that salvation is earned by what we do? Why or why not?

   APPLY: [Day 4, questions 8-10] Have you ever benefited spiritually from the ministry of someone who later turned out to be a false prophet? Describe that time. How did that experience change the way you viewed people in ministry? How did it change the way you viewed God?

4. **REFLECT:** [Day 5, questions 2-3] How are the two houses in Jesus' illustration similar? How are they different? At what point would the difference(s) be revealed between the two houses?

   APPLY: [Day 5, questions 5-6] What are some examples of rain, flood, and wind that come into our lives? Are these events always unexpected, uninvited, or undeserved? Describe a time in which someone's faith was revealed through a severe storm.

WRAP-UP: What impacted you most in this week's passage from the Sermon on the Mount? What are the words of Jesus asking of you personally?

VIDEO

Watch the teaching video for Week 9. Use the space below to take notes.

NOTES

Even the best moments

When

[ ] The narrow road is not about what you are
choosing but about what you are because
& the Lord always cares more about the
decisions.

L The narrow path is about becoming a person
who is .

An external appearance of goodness

After the video concludes, close your study in prayer. Praise God for the faithful record of Jesus' words in Matthew 5–7. Thank Him for the firm foundation they represent. Ask God to help you build the house of your faith into a dwelling fit for the Lord Himself. Ask Him to help you remember your own amazement at what the Sermon on the Mount contains, and to be changed by it. Thank God that Jesus lived out the "deeper obedience" of His sermon, as both our perfect example and our perfect atoning sacrifice. Thank Him that though the grass withers and the flowers fade, the Word of the Lord stands forever (see Isa. 40:8).

APPENDIX: MATTHEW 5-7

MATTHEW 5

¹ *Seeing the crowds, he went up on the mountain, and when he sat down, his disciples came to him.*

² *And he opened his mouth and taught them, saying:*

³ *"Blessed are the poor in spirit, for theirs is the kingdom of heaven.*

⁴ *"Blessed are those who mourn, for they shall be comforted.*

⁵ *"Blessed are the meek, for they shall inherit the earth.*

⁶ *"Blessed are those who hunger and thirst for righteousness, for they shall be satisfied.*

⁷ *"Blessed are the merciful, for they shall receive mercy.*

⁸ *"Blessed are the pure in heart, for they shall see God.*

⁹ *"Blessed are the peacemakers, for they shall be called sons of God.*

¹⁰ *"Blessed are those who are persecuted for righteousness' sake, for theirs is the kingdom of heaven.*

¹¹ *"Blessed are you when others revile you and persecute you and utter all kinds of evil against you falsely on my account.* ¹² *Rejoice and be glad, for your reward is great in heaven, for so they persecuted the prophets who were before you.*

¹³ *"You are the salt of the earth, but if salt has lost its taste, how shall its saltiness be restored? It is no longer good for anything except to be thrown out and trampled under people's feet.*

¹⁴*"You are the light of the world. A city set on a hill cannot be hidden.* ¹⁵ *Nor do people light a lamp and put it under a basket, but on a stand, and it gives light to all in the house.* ¹⁶ *In the same way, let your light shine before others, so that they may see your good works and give glory to your Father who is in heaven.*

17 "Do not think that I have come to abolish the Law or the Prophets; I have not come to abolish them but to fulfill them. 18 For truly, I say to you, until heaven and earth pass away, not an iota, not a dot, will pass from the Law until all is accomplished. 19 Therefore whoever relaxes one of the least of these commandments and teaches others to do the same will be called least in the kingdom of heaven, but whoever does them and teaches them will be called great in the kingdom of heaven. 20 For I tell you, unless your righteousness exceeds that of the scribes and Pharisees, you will never enter the kingdom of heaven.

21 "You have heard that it was said to those of old, 'You shall not murder; and whoever murders will be liable to judgment.' 22 But I say to you that everyone who is angry with his brother will be liable to judgment; whoever insults his brother will be liable to the council; and whoever says, 'You fool!' will be liable to the hell of fire. 23 So if you are offering your gift at the altar and there remember that your brother has something against you, 24 leave your gift there before the altar and go. First be reconciled to your brother, and then come and offer your gift. 25 Come to terms quickly with your accuser while you are going with him to court, lest your accuser hand you over to the judge, and the judge to the guard, and you be put in prison. 26 Truly, I say to you, you will never get out until you have paid the last penny.

27 "You have heard that it was said, 'You shall not commit adultery.' 28 But I say to you that everyone who looks at a woman with lustful intent has already committed adultery with her in his heart. 29 If your right eye causes you to sin, tear it out and throw it away. For it is better that you lose one of your members than that your whole body be thrown into hell. 30 And if your right hand causes you to sin, cut it off and throw it away. For it is better that you lose one of your members than that your whole body go into hell.

[31] *"It was also said, 'Whoever divorces his wife, let him give her a certificate of divorce.'* [32] *But I say to you that everyone who divorces his wife, except on the ground of sexual immorality, makes her commit adultery, and whoever marries a divorced woman commits adultery.*

[33] *"Again you have heard that it was said to those of old, 'You shall not swear falsely, but shall perform to the Lord what you have sworn.'* [34] *But I say to you, Do not take an oath at all, either by heaven, for it is the throne of God,* [35] *or by the earth, for it is his footstool, or by Jerusalem, for it is the city of the great King.* [36] *And do not take an oath by your head, for you cannot make one hair white or black.* [37] *Let what you say be simply 'Yes' or 'No'; anything more than this comes from evil.*

[38] *"You have heard that it was said, 'An eye for an eye and a tooth for a tooth.'* [39] *But I say to you, Do not resist the one who is evil. But if anyone slaps you on the right cheek, turn to him the other also.* [40] *And if anyone would sue you and take your tunic, let him have your cloak as well.* [41] *And if anyone forces you to go one mile, go with him two miles.* [42] *Give to the one who begs from you, and do not refuse the one who would borrow from you.*

[43] *"You have heard that it was said, 'You shall love your neighbor and hate your enemy.'* [44] *But I say to you, Love your enemies and pray for those who persecute you,* [45] *so that you may be sons of your Father who is in heaven. For he makes his sun rise on the evil and on the good, and sends rain on the just and on the unjust.* [46] *For if you love those who love you, what reward do you have? Do not even the tax collectors do the same?* [47] *And if you greet only your brothers, what more are you doing than others? Do not even the Gentiles do the same?* [48] *You therefore must be perfect, as your heavenly Father is perfect.*

MATTHEW 6

[1] *"Beware of practicing your righteousness before other people in order to be seen by them, for then you will have no reward from your Father who is in heaven.*

[2] *"Thus, when you give to the needy, sound no trumpet before you, as the hypocrites do in the synagogues and in the streets, that they may be praised by others. Truly, I say to you, they have received their reward.* [3] *But when you give to the needy, do not let your left hand know what your right hand is doing,* [4] *so that your giving may be in secret. And your Father who sees in secret will reward you.*

[5] *"And when you pray, you must not be like the hypocrites. For they love to stand and pray in the synagogues and at the street corners, that they may be seen by others. Truly, I say to you, they have received their reward.* [6] *But when you pray, go into your room and shut the door and pray to your Father who is in secret. And your Father who sees in secret will reward you.*

[7] *"And when you pray, do not heap up empty phrases as the Gentiles do, for they think that they will be heard for their many words.* [8] *Do not be like them, for your Father knows what you need before you ask him.* [9] *Pray then like this:*

> *"Our Father in heaven,*
>   *hallowed be your name.*
>   [10] *Your kingdom come,*
>   *your will be done,*
>   *on earth as it is in heaven.*
>   [11] *Give us this day our daily bread,*
>   [12] *and forgive us our debts,*
>   *as we also have forgiven our debtors.*
>   [13] *And lead us not into temptation,*
>   *but deliver us from evil.*

[14] For if you forgive others their trespasses, your heavenly Father will also forgive you,

[15] but if you do not forgive others their trespasses, neither will your Father forgive your trespasses.

[16] "And when you fast, do not look gloomy like the hypocrites, for they disfigure their faces that their fasting may be seen by others. Truly, I say to you, they have received their reward. [17] But when you fast, anoint your head and wash your face, [18] that your fasting may not be seen by others but by your Father who is in secret. And your Father who sees in secret will reward you.

[19] "Do not lay up for yourselves treasures on earth, where moth and rust destroy and where thieves break in and steal, [20] but lay up for yourselves treasures in heaven, where neither moth nor rust destroys and where thieves do not break in and steal. [21] For where your treasure is, there your heart will be also.

[22] "The eye is the lamp of the body. So, if your eye is healthy, your whole body will be full of light, [23] but if your eye is bad, your whole body will be full of darkness. If then the light in you is darkness, how great is the darkness!

[24] "No one can serve two masters, for either he will hate the one and love the other, or he will be devoted to the one and despise the other. You cannot serve God and money.

[25] "Therefore I tell you, do not be anxious about your life, what you will eat or what you will drink, nor about your body, what you will put on. Is not life more than food, and the body more than clothing? [26] Look at the birds of the air: they neither sow nor reap nor gather into barns, and yet your heavenly Father feeds them. Are you not of more value than they? [27] And which of you by being anxious can add a single hour to his span of life? [28] And why are you anxious about clothing? Consider the lilies of the field, how they grow: they neither toil nor spin, [29] yet I tell you, even Solomon in all his glory was not arrayed like one of these. [30] But if God so clothes the grass of the field, which today is alive and tomorrow is thrown into the oven, will he not much more clothe you, O you of little faith? [31] Therefore do not be anxious, saying, 'What shall we eat?' or 'What shall we

drink?' or 'What shall we wear?' [32] For the Gentiles seek after all these things, and your heavenly Father knows that you need them all. [33] But seek first the kingdom of God and his righteousness, and all these things will be added to you.

[34] "Therefore do not be anxious about tomorrow, for tomorrow will be anxious for itself. Sufficient for the day is its own trouble.

MATTHEW 7

[1] "Judge not, that you be not judged. [2] For with the judgment you pronounce you will be judged, and with the measure you use it will be measured to you. [3] Why do you see the speck that is in your brother's eye, but do not notice the log that is in your own eye? [4] Or how can you say to your brother, 'Let me take the speck out of your eye,' when there is the log in your own eye? [5] You hypocrite, first take the log out of your own eye, and then you will see clearly to take the speck out of your brother's eye.

[6] "Do not give dogs what is holy, and do not throw your pearls before pigs, lest they trample them underfoot and turn to attack you.

[7] "Ask, and it will be given to you; seek, and you will find; knock, and it will be opened to you. [8] For everyone who asks receives, and the one who seeks finds, and to the one who knocks it will be opened. [9] Or which one of you, if his son asks him for bread, will give him a stone? [10] Or if he asks for a fish, will give him a serpent? [11] If you then, who are evil, know how to give good gifts to your children, how much more will your Father who is in heaven give good things to those who ask him!

[12] "So whatever you wish that others would do to you, do also to them, for this is the Law and the Prophets.

[13] "Enter by the narrow gate. For the gate is wide and the way easy that leads to destruction, and those who enter by it are many. [14] For the gate is narrow and the way is hard that leads to life, and those who find it are few.

[15] "Beware of false prophets, who come to you in sheep's clothing but inwardly are ravenous wolves. [16] You will recognize them by their fruits. Are grapes gathered from thornbushes, or figs from thistles? [17] So, every healthy tree bears good fruit, but the diseased tree bears bad fruit. [18] A healthy tree cannot bear bad fruit, nor can a diseased tree bear good fruit. [19] Every tree that does not bear good fruit is cut down and thrown into the fire. [20] Thus you will recognize them by their fruits.

[21] "Not everyone who says to me, 'Lord, Lord,' will enter the kingdom of heaven, but the one who does the will of my Father who is in heaven. [22] On that day many will say to me, 'Lord, Lord, did we not prophesy in your name, and cast out demons in your name, and do many mighty works in your name?' [23] And then will I declare to them, 'I never knew you; depart from me, you workers of lawlessness.'

[24] "Everyone then who hears these words of mine and does them will be like a wise man who built his house on the rock. [25] And the rain fell, and the floods came, and the winds blew and beat on that house, but it did not fall, because it had been founded on the rock. [26] And everyone who hears these words of mine and does not do them will be like a foolish man who built his house on the sand. [27] And the rain fell, and the floods came, and the winds blew and beat against that house, and it fell, and great was the fall of it."

[28] And when Jesus finished these sayings, the crowds were astonished at his teaching, [29] for he was teaching them as one who had authority, and not as their scribes.